FOOD FOR A JOURNEY

Poems by

Tom Gannon

Antrim House
Simsbury, Connecticut

Library of Congress Control Number: 2015947144

ISBN: 978-1-936482-33-7

First Edition, 2015

Printed & bound by United Graphics, LLC

Book design by Rennie McQuilkin

Front cover and inner title page artwork
by the author

Author photograph by Kate Gannon

Antrim House
860.217.0023
AntrimHouse@comcast.net
www.AntrimHouseBooks.com
21 Goodrich Road, Simsbury, CT 06070

It is difficult to put into words all that my wife Ann and my children Mark and Kate have meant to me and have given to me over so many years, but the publication of this book provides the opportunity to say "thank you" in a very public way. Ann, Mark, and Kate, *Food for a Journey* is for you.

ACKNOWLEDGMENTS

Almost all of these poems draw on my own personal experience, but as I was only fifteen years old during the climactic battle of the First Indochina War, the poem entitled "Adventuress" required a fair amount of research. The principal books I consulted were Bernard Fall's *Street Without Joy* and *Hell in a Very Small Place,* Jules Roy's *The Battle of Dienbienphu,* Ted Morgan's *Valley of Death,* and Martin Windrow's *The Last Valley.* In addition, for the poem entitled "Changing Times," I supplemented my own personal recollections of the 1968 Democratic National Convention by consulting *An American Melodrama: The Presidential Campaign of 1968,* by Lewis Chester, Godfrey Hodgson, and Bruce Page.

SPECIAL THANKS

There are so many people to thank for inspiration, instruction, and encouragement along the road to this publication: my late parents, Eleanor Agnes Lavin and Thomas Michael Gannon Sr., who first instilled a love of learning; my siblings, John and Marie who are still with us, Jim and Jerry who are not, all of whom were, or continue to be, immensely supportive of their oldest brother.

On the writing side specifically, there were the Immaculate Heart nuns at St. Edmond's who taught me to diagram a sentence; the St. Joe's Prep faculty members who required a written composition every single week; the late Frank O'Malley who at Notre Dame gave me some hope of becoming a half-decent writer; Barrie Maguire, Notre Dame classmate and source of artistic inspiration; the late Henry Lavin, S.J., who introduced me to John Donne, Andrew Marvell, and George Herbert; the late Don Campion, S.J., who brought me onto the *America* staff and published so much of my work; the late A. Leon Higginbotham, Jr., civil rights leader, federal judge, great man; Ken Ludwig, law firm colleague, super-successful playwright, and source of literary inspiration; and Natasha Karpinskaia, whose printmaking workshops led to the image on this book's cover.

More immediately, I am ever so grateful to Genevieve and Wayne Lalle, who introduced me to Antrim House author Pat O'Brien, who in turn introduced me to Rennie McQuilkin, Antrim House's publisher, whose shrewd advice, boundless energy, and steadfast devotion to poetry have been beyond invaluable in making the publication of *Food for a Journey* a reality.

I'm sure I've missed some. I am very grateful to them too.

TABLE OF CONTENTS

As a writing man, or secretary, I have always felt charged with the safekeeping of all unexpected items of worldly or unworldly enchantment, as though I might be held personally responsible if even a small one were lost.

– E. B. White, *The Points of My Compass*

FOOD FOR A JOURNEY

I. NEIGHBORHOOD

Indifference

A rowhouse in South Philly,
Home of cheesesteaks and hoagies,
Phillies and Flyers and Eagles.
The front steps, cement, four of them
Shared with the house next door.
An enclosed porch, mostly window,
Unheated, cold in the winter.
Below it, two small windows,
Set into the russet brick face of the cellar,
Each with its black metal grate.
The windows open only once or twice a year,
When the coal truck rumbles up and
Backs onto the sidewalk.
My mother opens a window from within.
The driver pulls a grate aside,
Inserts the tongue of his chute
Through the open window
So the coal will flow
Into the bin below.
He pulls a lever and the coal begins to pour,
Thousands of black chunks, a ton of them,
Down the chute and into the bin,
There to rest, quiet, dirty, dusty,
Until my father shovels it
Into the furnace's fiery mouth
On cold winter nights.

It is my earliest memory.
I cannot explain why it stays with me,
But it does.

The grates on the cellar windows,
They are central to it.
I had had, I guessed, a soft childhood,
The cosseted first-born.

I was on the sidewalk
In front of our house that day
At play with other children.
(Our street teemed with children in those days
When V-mails arrived from an uncle at Anzio.)
Did I trip or was I pushed?
It could have been a push.
Some of the neighborhood children
Thought a push from behind a fun thing.
I do not remember, and it does not matter.
Whatever the cause,
I found myself hurtling, face first,
Towards the cellar windows and their black grates.
Face met grate,
The grate hard, rigid, unyielding,
And with the pain,
Not much pain, but enough,
Came insight:
This small world of mine,
It was not what I thought it to be.

Cloistered Life

Every Italian household had one,
Or so it seemed,
To her grandson's classmates at least:
An older woman,
Small, bent, wizened,
Gray hair pulled back in a bun,
Clad all in black,
A filmy tunic over a long dress
That an Italian noblewoman
Might have worn a century before.
She hovered in the semi-darkness
Beyond the living room
When guests arrived,
Soon to retreat into the kitchen,
Where her spiced tomato gravy
(Her people did not call it "sauce")
Simmered on the stove –
Smiling warily, timidly,
The smile not quite natural,
Not so much forced as
Produced because expected,
Mute in the presence of visitors
Because she had no English and
They had no Italian.

Far removed from bomb-wrecked Naples and
Its twisting, garbage-strewn lanes, or
A hardscrabble farm in the bleak Calabrian hills, or
A tiny flat among Palermo's swaggering gangsters.
She had been brought over after the war and

The collapse of Il Duce's imperial fantasy,
Brought over to join her children,
The venturesome ones
Who had already established themselves
In the New World,
In William Penn's fair city
On the west bank of the Delaware.

It was a cloistered life to be sure,
Enclosed by lack of language,
Cooking and cleaning
For children and grandchildren.
But the work was not a burden.
She had always worked
Before the voyage to America,
From the time she was a little girl.
Not for her to sit all day
In an upholstered easy chair,
Dreaming, perhaps even fondly,
Of the life she had left behind,
Of those years in Naples or Calabria or Palermo.

It was not a perfect life
In this new and unfamiliar world
Of a South Philadelphia rowhouse,
But better, a life without the hunger and fear
She had known for so long,
Safe at last in a refuge
She had not known existed,
Smiling so warily, so timidly,
Out of semi-darkness,
At her grandson's classmates.

Business Venture

I

The space had been empty for many months,
But the two men thought they could use it
For the furniture store they had dreamed of owning.
The great department stores were extending
Their tentacles downwards,
Anchoring a mall a dozen blocks away.
But the two men saw advantage in their chosen site.
A corner location in a crowded rowhouse neighborhood,
Three large display windows fronting the avenue that ran past,
A fourth facing the cross street.

No shortage of traffic,
The avenue a main east-west route,
Trackless trolleys stopping on two corners
Of the intersection's four.
Plenty of pedestrians too,
With a popular bakery a block to the south,
The neighborhood pharmacy even closer on the west,
A Methodist church across the street, and
A Catholic church, big as an indoor stadium,
With thousands of parishioners fifty yards away.

So the two men signed the lease,
Filled the showroom with the goods they hoped to sell,
Armchairs and sofas and dining room sets,
Beds in variety, kings and queens and twins.
Fearing the bleaching of upholstery by the afternoon sun,
They covered the display windows with cellophane
Tinted with see-through orange.
And then they waited
For customers to appear.

II

The altar boy passed the store dozens of times
During business hours.
In mid-morning on weekdays
On his way to serve funeral Masses,
A welcome respite from the Seventh Grade grind
Of vocabulary drills and exercise in mental arithmetic,
The Masses taking precedence over English and math.
On Saturday mornings too, the most prized assignment of all,
When there were nuptial Masses to be served and
In the sacristy before Mass, as the groom paced nervously,
The best man pulled out a roll of bills and
Peeled off a ten for each of the servers.
On Saturday afternoons too, every other week,
While scraping his conscience for sins to confess
At the indoor stadium down the street.

Each time the boy passed the store,
He glanced within,
And in every glance
He saw the same two men,
Sitting in two of their ready-for-sale armchairs,
Bathed in thin orange light,
Chatting idly, waiting for the customers
Who never seemed to appear.
Even then, when the boy was – what? Thirteen? –
He sensed what the men in the armchairs were feeling.
Failure was what they were sensing.
The department stores had won.
Dispiriting, even for a thirteen-year-old,
Who was not surprised when,
After a period of months,
The furniture had disappeared and
The space was empty again.

Teaching Method

Four years of it,
First home room, with the beadle
Busy with housekeeping.
Then Latin, always the first period,
And always, every morning
Regular as clockwork
At the beginning of the period,
The black-cassocked teacher,
Priest or scholastic,
Issued the marching order,
"Take out a half-sheet."
Had the quiz been ordained by the Founder,
The redoubtable Ignatius of Loyola, or
Did it only seem that way?

The fundamentals in freshman year,
Vir, viri, femina, feminae,
Man and men, woman and women.
Sum, es, est, sumus, estis, sunt.
I am, you are, he is (or she is),
We are, you are (again, but more of you), they are.
Amo, amas, amat, amamus, amatis, amant.
All the loves, so favored by crossword makers.

Progress to three-parted Gaul in sophomore year,
With Caesar the proconsul,
The Helvetii and the Suevi and the Belgae,
Vercingetorix, chief of the Arverni,
The great cataract of gerundives as
The Romans wade ashore in Britain,
An Omaha Beach in reverse.

Politics in junior year,
With Cicero, golden-tongued consul,
Confronting the conspiratorial,
Patience-abusing Catiline
On the floor of the Senate.

And finally, in senior year,
Aeneas the True, as one translator calls him,
In flight with his household gods
From the treacherous Greeks and the wily Ulysses.
Among the dramatis personae, the faithful Achates,
Palinurus the drowned helmsman,
Aeneas's lover, the unhappy, suicidal Dido, and
The Cumaean Sibyl, who would lead Aeneas
Through the Underworld,
As Virgil himself would lead Dante.

And always, regardless of subject matter,
The rudiments of grammar, the war story,
The oration, the epic poem,
The teacher's command,
"Take out a half-sheet."
No surprises in the questions.
All covered the day before
In the prelection.
Ten new vocabulary words,
A sentence of lofty Roman rhetoric,
Two lines of dactylic hexameter.
Not a high bar to get over.
A few moments of study the night before,
All it would take
To fix the material in the mind,
Prime the pump of adolescent memory.

Tell them,
The boys and girls in
The schools that are failing,
Tell them, every morning,
"Take out a half-sheet."
The matters they are quizzed on
Will stay with them.
Bet on it.
"Take out a half-sheet."

Escalation

It begins innocently enough.
Two teams of teenage football players,
Neither big enough nor good enough
To play for their high school varsities,
But willing, even eager,
To play on a Sunday afternoon,
Bright with mid-October sunshine.
Clad in sandlot motley,
A rainbow array of patched jerseys,
Jeans rather than football pants,
Cracked, mud-streaked football shoes,
Their cleats worn down to nubs.
Without officials, penalties on the honor system
On the yellowed grass and
Brown, hard-packed earth
Of a field in a public park.

At the start, all is well,
The players lifted in spirit by
The sheer joy of competing.
But one team soon is dominating,
Three touchdowns in quick succession.
No quit in their opponents, though,
Who dispatch runners to their home neighborhoods,
Summoning reinforcements
Who soon turn the tide of battle.
The other team responds in kind, and
The original players on both sides
Are reduced to spectators as
Older, bigger, stronger boys replace them.

The game takes on a new seriousness,
The honor system collapses, and
The uncalled infractions – holding,
Clipping, pass interference – multiply.

Pushing and shoving follow, and
Before the impending brawl commences,
Each side chooses a champion
To settle the issue, medieval style,
In single combat.
On one side, a blond youngster,
Small but compact, muscular, fearless,
Nicknamed "Panther" for his ferocity.
On the other, a much bigger boy,
A giant really, but a gentle one,
Not so heavily muscled, and
No streetfighter.

No Marquess of Queensbury rules in this bout,
Which ends in seconds.
The Panther ducks under his opponent's punches,
Hooks a foot behind one of his foe's, and
Spins the bigger boy to the ground.
Before his opponent can scramble to his feet,
The Panther raises his cleated foot and
Stomps on the bigger boy's face.
Blood flows copiously –
Face cuts are like that –
In twisting, bright-red rivulets,
Down the bigger boy's face,
Dripping onto his jersey
As he struggles to his feet.
The Panther steps back,

Ready to resume the fight,
But his opponent has had enough.
Among the onlookers, a consensus develops:
Honor has been satisfied.

Another sunny Sunday afternoon
On the playing fields of South Philadelphia.
The original players drift away
Before the police arrive.

The Man: A Memory

A mid-fifties baseball bargain,
Two games for the price of one.
A twilight-night doubleheader in mid-July,
The Cardinals at the Phillies.

In the first game, a double treat.
Two immortals-to-be, on their roads to the Hall of Fame,
Robin Roberts on the mound for the Phils
And for the Cards, playing first base, batting third,
Stanley Frank Musial, "Stan the Man."

The subway ride north, beneath Broad Street,
Avenue to avenue, Snyder to Lehigh,
The walk west from the subway, out Lehigh Avenue,
Part of a human tide of thousands,
Past the peddlers of caps and buttons and pennants.

The ball park rising out of the rowhouse neighborhood,
Bathed in the warm, late-afternoon glow,
The sun setting behind the upper deck
That looks down on third base.

In their white summer uniform shirts and caps,
The traffic cops stand tall, controlling the ballpark bustle,
Rumored to permit parking in choice but illegal spaces
In return for a small gratuity.

A short line at the ticket window,
Then passage through the turnstiles,
Clutching the stub the ushers will want to see.
A climb up a flight of stairs

To the concourse behind the lower deck seats
That slope gently down to the field.
A few more steps and
Opening out below, the field itself.

A pause, a moment of awe.
It is like entering sacred space,
An open-air cathedral of sport,
The awe inspired not by statuary
Or mosaics or stained glass,
But by the very greenness of the grass.
Has God ever made grass any greener
Than the outfield grass at a big league ballpark?

Another climb, to upper deck seats
Far down the right field line.
Not great seats, no, but good enough.

The first game close into the seventh inning,
Roberts yielding a run,
But the Phils have scored two.
In the top of the seventh, though, trouble.
Two Cardinals reach base and then,
With two out, Musial steps into the batter's box,
Assumes the tense, coiled, crouching stance that
A coach memorably describes as
"A kid peeking around the corner
To see if the cops are coming," and
Waits for the first Roberts pitch.
Thus the duel begins, but soon it is over.
A Roberts pitch is on the way and
Musial likes its look.
He uncoils from his crouch.
Bat meets ball with a sharp crack and

The ball rockets through the warm July air
Towards the gap in right center field.
"Open spaces, extra bases,"
As the play-by-play announcers say.
No fly ball this. More like the mother of all line drives.

The ball smacks again the base of the right field wall,
Skitters away.
Before the Phillies' outfielders can run it down,
Two runs score and Musial stands on second base.
Roberts pitches valiantly through the ninth,
But the Man's double is the game-winner.

In the second game, the Phillies' rightfielder,
Homegrown hero Del Ennis,
In a feeble imitation of the basket catch
Made famous by Willie Mays,
Muffs a routine fly ball with the bases loaded.
Three Cardinals score, and
The boos roll down from the stands.
This is, after all, Philadelphia.

An inning later, redemption.
After the Phils load the bases,
Ennis steps up to the plate and
Calmly drives a fastball
Towards the roof of the left field grandstand.
The ball hits the sloping front face of the roof,
Bounces into the air and over the roof
Into the darkness of the North Philadelphia night.
Four runs score, the roar of the crowd deafening.
Crowds are volatile.

Another Saturday night at the ballpark.
The Ennis home run a dramatic moment,
More dramatic than the Musial double,
But that line-drive double,
Almost sixty years later
Upon the death of the Man,
Is a memory still to be treasured.

II. MATTERS OF FAITH

Cigarette Man

They have come a long way,
These small, brown men
From Guatemala and El Salvador,
From Puerto Rico and the Dominican,
To the gloomy common room of
This county prison in
The Pennsylvania Dutch country,
Men of small crimes
That match their stature,
Caught up in a system
Whose language they barely
Understand and cannot speak.
Confined within the system's
Regime of punishment for their offenses,
They cluster together, a dozen or so,
In a corner of the common room,
Confined by language as well.

Seminarians the Anglo prisoners call "the brothers"
Make twice-weekly visits to the prison,
But they cannot pierce the isolation of
The small brown men.
The brothers have no Spanish,
And the small brown men
Have no English.

Placido too has come a long way,
From a house of studies in his native Spain
To this American seminary
Nestled in the rolling Pennsylvania hills,
But he is only passing through,

A pilgrim of sorts
On his way to the order's mission in Japan,
The purpose of his visit
A month's immersion in English,
The everyday language in the order's
Multi-national houses in Japan.

Placido is popular with the Americans,
Small, wiry, intense,
Not unlike the Hispanic prisoners.
He is spry as a cricket,
A blur on the soccer field
With the ball at his feet, and
Above all, for the brothers
Who visit the prison,
A speaker of Spanish.
They invite him to join them
On their next prison visit.
He does not hesitate,
Welcomes the chance
To speak his own language
For a few hours a week,
A break from the strain of
His struggle with English.

The brothers warn him
The Hispanic prisoners are distant,
Wary behind the barrier of language.
Placido is not worried.
He knows a tactic,
An ice-breaker of sorts.
He visited prisons
As a seminarian in Spain, and

The tactic worked there.
Why not in America too?

A request is made to a seminary superior,
Granted because Placido is older,
Further along in his studies
Than the younger men
Who regularly visit the prison.
He can be trusted.
A visit to the storeroom
Where tobacco products are kept
For the few remaining faculty smokers,
A brief search, and Placido emerges
With a carton of Lucky Strikes.

Placido enters the common room
With the seminarians on their next visit,
Spies the Hispanic inmates
Gathered in their customary corner,
Marches over, surprises them by
Addressing them familiarly in their own language.
Their attention captured,
He promptly wins them entirely over
By producing from within his cassock
The carton of Lucky Strikes.

For the next several weeks
He sits in the midst of the Hispanic prisoners,
Chattering away with them,
The smoke from the cigarettes
He continues to bring
Rising around him.
A modest gesture of respect, of kindness,

Makes him the most popular seminarian
Ever to visit the prison.

Brothers and prisoners alike
Mourn his departure for Japan, and
The brothers ponder the mystery:
Who would have thought that
The path to a prisoner's soul
Might lead through his lungs?

Counseling Session

"CCD," they call it,
Catholic shorthand
for Confraternity of Christian Doctrine
(Whatever a confraternity is),
Part of American Catholicism's
Modest bowl of alphabet soup,
Religious instruction for Catholic children
Not enrolled in parochial schools,
Released for an hour
From their public schools
In the middle of the school day,
A church-state accommodation.
The children are registered by parents
Keeping a marital promise to raise their children
In the One True Faith.

In this middle-class suburban community,
The CCD teachers are seminarians,
Aspirants for the priesthood
In their early to mid-twenties,
Grateful for contact with human beings
Other than faculty members and each other.
Welcoming the weekly escape
From the seminary's isolation and
Its intellectual universe of bleak abstraction,
Philosophy courses, so many of them
Channeling Aristotle through Thomas Aquinas –
Essence and existence,
Matter and form,
Substance and accident.
Ontology and epistemology,

Cosmology and natural theology
Compressed into triple theses
Hundreds of years old.
Only a few professors, the daring ones,
Gingerly present insights
From European phenomenology,
From Marcel and Heidegger and Merleau-Ponty,
Wondering if Rome will object.

The highlight of the CCD program:
Individual counseling sessions,
Personal contact with students
Beyond the religious instruction
In which the students show little interest.
"Leave the session open," the director says:
"Whatever they want to talk about,
Whatever is on their minds."

A seminarian anticipates his first interview
With a member of his Eighth Grade class.
He thinks of the problems
The young man may face,
Problems that may rise to the surface
In a free-flowing counseling session –
An alcoholic father,
A mother sunk in depression,
A tyrannical teacher,
The torments of adolescent sexuality,
Even obstacles to belief in God.

Visions of famed spiritual conversations
Flood his mind –
Ambrose converting Augustine,
Ignatius Loyola inspiring Francis Xavier.

Who knows? This may be another
In that long, graced line.

The student – blond, sharp-featured,
Lean, wiry, athletic, thirteen years old –
Responds without hesitation
To the seminarians's invitation
To say what is on his mind.
"There is one thing," the boy says.
The seminarian catches his breath,
Alert for a revelation.
"See, I'm a runner," the boy says.
"And if I can just get my time
For the eight hundred
Down to two-ten
That would be big, really big."
"Two-ten?" the seminarian asks, puzzled.
"Two minutes, ten seconds," the boy explains.
"My time. For eight hundred meters.
I'm at two-twenty now,
But I know I can do better."
"Oh. Yes," the seminarian says,
Feeling, not for the first time,
An other-worldly fool.

So, no alcoholic father or
Depressed mother or tyrannical teacher or
Teen-aged sexual angst.
No great crisis of faith or morals,
No dark night of the adolescent soul.
Two-ten in the eight hundred meters,
At thirteen, all that really matters.
Something big, really big.

Food for a Journey

The priest is a beginner at this thing,
This business of being a priest.
He has been ordained for less than three months.
He helps to edit a magazine,
Deals with words, sentences, paragraphs,
With people not so much.
He wants, he needs experience,
Experience with people,
Experiences as a priest
Working with people.

An opportunity arises.
Two weeks in a hospital,
A substitute for one of two chaplains.
The novice priest volunteers,
Takes up the duties of the man he replaces,
Dividing responsibility for the patients' floors
With the chaplain who remains.

The novice priest finds there are things he can do:
Offer Mass, give Communion to the bed-ridden,
Hear confessions (not many of those),
Pray with those who want to be prayed with.
Some do not want his ministrations;
They make that very clear.
He skips their rooms as he makes his rounds.

He finds there are some things he cannot do.
He does not have the words to console a single mother
Who has lost her four-year-old son,
The center of her life, to a wasting disease.

In his inadequacy,
The novice priest offers his presence.
Perhaps that is something.
The woman knows no other priests.
She asks him to offer her son's funeral Mass.
He does that readily.
Perhaps that is something too.

Neither can he find the words
To comfort a young woman
Raped by a pretended friend
Days after she arrives in the city.
Again, in his inadequacy,
The novice priest offers his presence.
Perhaps that is something.
In an emergency room corridor, detectives confer
With the doctor who will examine the victim
For evidence of the crime.
The novice priest wonders if the moral theologians
Would approve of a D and C.

Patients come and go.
One comes and stays, in a private room
On the floor the nurses call the Gold Coast.
He is the most famous football coach in America.
He has colon cancer, and he is very ill.
The novice priest does not see him –
The other chaplain has responsibility for the fifth floor –
But he sees the coach's former players
When they come to visit,
Huge men filling hospital corridors with their bulk.
Men black, white, whatever,
Packer green and gold the only colors that mattered.
They leave the hospital shaken.

The man who led them,
whose will drove them to championships,
is in decline.
The coach's employer visits with them;
He is the most famous trial lawyer in America,
Defender of Joe McCarthy, Frank Costello, and Jimmy Hoffa,
But he cannot defend the coach from the cancer.

It is Sunday night
The other chaplain is away.
The novice priest has responsibility for the entire hospital.
He makes his evening rounds and this time
The coach is on his list for Communion.
It is not surprising.
When he was well, the coach went to Mass,
Received Communion every day.

The novice priest approaches the coach's room,
Knocks with some trepidation.
His contact with legends has been limited.
The coach's wife comes to the door.
She shakes her head.
The coach is having a blood transfusion.
He cannot receive Communion.
The novice priest moves on, to the next floor.

He is still there when a nurse appears –
She has an urgent summons.
"Father," she says, "you have to come back to the coach's room.
When he found out that his wife had sent you away,
He hit the roof."
The roof-hitting is easily imagined.
All those televised sideline eruptions

At his own erring players, at hapless referees.
The novice priest assures the nurse he will return.

Outside the coach's room,
His wife slumps on a bench, chastened.
Inside, the room is fragrant, flower-filled.
So many flowers from so many people.
The coach is sitting up in bed.

He may be wasted by illness,
But he still projects an immense personal force.
He speaks to the novice priest in the rasping voice
That millions would recognize.
"We had some trouble, Father,
But we got that straightened out."

The novice priest takes a host
From his pyx, the gold-leaf-lined vessel
In which the chaplains bring
Communion to patients.
The host is not large,
A thin, dry, tasteless wafer
Of unleavened bread
The size of a quarter.
But when the coach sees it, he waves it off.
He has trouble swallowing.
For him, the host is too large.

The novice priest breaks off a piece,
A sliver of unleavened bread
A quarter of an inch wide.
Small enough for the coach to receive and swallow,
Food for the next stage of his journey,
One that will not end at a fifty-yard line.

The novice priest places the fragment
on the coach's tongue.
A glass of water helps him to swallow it.
He thanks the novice priest,
Who gives the coach his blessing and departs in a daze.

The novice priest's two weeks of experience,
Experience as a priest
Working with people,
Come to an end.
He returns to his magazine,
To words and sentences and paragraphs.

A few days later
The next stage of the coach's journey begins.

On Retreat

A college campus
Near the end of August
Largely deserted,
Summer school over,
The fall semester not yet begun,
Quiet, peaceful,
Traffic noises muffled, distant,
A suitable site
For prayer, for reflection.

The retreatant's name is Paul.
He and his director meet
In a barren college dorm room,
Paul's home for the next eight days.

Paul's desire is a good retreat,
One whose effects will last
More than a few weeks,
Unlike those of so many other retreats
In his twelve years of religious life:
Heightened fervor
Soon succeeded by regression
Into the mild piety of the past.

To that end he resolves:
No questions about God's existence.
He will not spend eight days
Wondering if when he prays,
There is no one, as the French poet
Phrased it, "gladly listening,"
Wondering if what he perceives

As moments of grace
Are merely instances of self-suggestion,
Of cultural conditioning.
The thought has occurred to him
From time to time, over the years:
What if Freud was right?
What if all religion is an illusion?
Paul has suppressed the thought before and
He will suppress it again,
The retreat no time
For theological speculation.

The retreat's goal is simple,
A renewal of Paul's commitment
To follow Jesus Christ,
The retreat plan drafted centuries before
By a Sixteenth Century Basque nobleman
Crippled by a cannonball
During an obscure siege
In one of that century's little wars,
Converted from the pursuit of military glory
to another quest as
He lay abed recovering.

At their first meeting,
The director counsels patience, passivity –
"Allow God to act," he says to Paul.
"Expect surprise, even though
You do not know what it will be.
Let God show you what he has in mind,
Let it be a personal encounter,
Between you as you are and God as he is.
Take a chance on God," the director says.
"Embrace what God has in store for you.

Trust that God's project for you
Will be more exciting than
Any you can dream up on your own."

Strong meat, the crippled Basque's plan.
It encourages retreatants,
So long as it is God's will,
To desire earnestly,
To choose deliberately,
To imitate Christ in bearing
All wrongs, all abuse, all poverty,
To live with poverty rather than riches,
With insults and contempt rather than honor,
With humility rather than pride,
To be thought worthless and a fool for Christ
Rather than esteemed as wise and prudent.
Not entirely original, these sentiments.
An earlier Paul, once a Pharisee,
Wrote of the foolishness of God
And its wisdom,
Of the weakness of God
And its strength.

Paul is apprehensive.
Something will be asked of him.
The director counsels patience again,
Realism and honesty too:
"When you pray, say only what you want to say,
Only what you are given to say."

As the days pass slowly by
The mysteries of the Galilean's life unfold:
In three and four meditations a day,
Events, places, people:

Birth, infancy, public life,
Passion, death, resurrection;
Mary and Joseph, John the Baptist,
Peter the fisherman, Thomas the doubter,
Mary Magdalen, Judas the betrayer,
The high priests, the Pharisees and Sadducees, and
Pontius Pilate, the Roman procurator;
Bethlehem and Nazareth,
Cana and Capernaum,
Bethany and Jerusalem,
The River Jordan and the Sea of Galilee.

"Movements of the soul will come,"
the director says. Paul wonders what they will be.
He thinks of what life would be like
As an object of contempt,
Of insults, of rejection, of scorn
For his perceived foolishness.
Could he bear all of that,
Day after day, year after year,
So much for flesh to bear?
Too much, he fears, for his flesh.

He imagines an alternative future,
A future without the surrender of self
That is the object of the retreat.
An interior line drawn:
Yes to poverty
Yes to the contempt of others,
Yes to worthlessness,
Yes to a reputation for foolishness,
But not too much,
Nothing extreme.
All of this possible,

But within limits.
It cannot be limitless,
This surrender, this abandonment of self,
A self, a life even, constructed,
Formed with difficulty
Over a span of decades.

He does not think he can bear this loss,
Yield up the fortress of his self.

Early evening on the seventh day of the retreat.
The late summer day draws to a close,
The sun a white disk
Sinking behind a grove of trees to the west.
Paul walks slowly along the tree-shaded paths
Between the gray stone classroom buildings.
A slight breeze ripples the leaves overhead.

The retreat has not been wasted.
He sees his future more clearly now.
He will go on, finish the retreat,
Return to his assignment,
But he will cling to that last remnant of self.
He cannot let it go.
It is not much, this self of his,
But it is all he has.
He senses that if he gives up
This flawed, familiar self,
He will no longer know
Who he is, and
He shrinks from the prospect.

At the beginning of his religious life,
He was full of energy, enthusiasm.

He did not yet know who he was.
Now, after twelve years,
He knows better, and so
He will decline the offered invitation,
Will settle for something less,
Live in between,
Beyond conventional upright behavior,
But short of surrender, of entering upon
A life he no longer controls.
He will have his own self, and
That will have to be enough.
Not a bad life, just not the life
It might have been.
And if Freud was right,
If there is no one there,
No life beyond death,
Well, it will not matter, will it?

III. ON GUARD

Changing Times

I

It was very early on a Thursday morning,
Not long after midnight.
The hotel ballroom was mostly empty,
Its floor brightly lit, but no one was dancing.
Young men and women clustered in small groups
Around the ballroom's shadowed perimeter,
Talking in little more than whispers,
Shaken, in shock from what they had seen,
What the whole world would eventually see.
A young woman approached a piano,
Seated herself on the bench,
Addressed the keys, and
After so much had happened, began to play –

After it all began in the
Every-four-years-famous snows of New Hampshire,
With a senator from Minnesota
Improbably playing Don Quixote and
Hundreds of twenty-somethings
Playing Sancho Panza.

After the Viet Cong, supposedly in decline,
Had appeared in dozens of South Vietnamese cities
In a Tet Offensive that helped
To drive a President from office.

After the casualty figures rose
To four hundred dead Americans a week.

After the Yippies nominated a pig, and
The Chicago police solemnly arrested the pig.

After a band struck up "Chicago," and
The mayor of that toddling town
Bounced into a delegate reception
Like a giant jowly rubber ball,
Clad in tastefully-tailored light-gray pinstripes.

After the delegates first alighted from their buses
Outside the convention hall, and
The reek of animal blood
From the nearby stockyards
Assaulted their nostrils.
"Hog Butcher for the World,"
The poet had rightly written.

After the delegations from New York and California,
Strong for McCarthy or the second martyred Kennedy,
Were banished, like unruly children,
To the farthest reaches of the convention floor
To be seen and not heard.

After battles over credentials
Between party regulars and insurgents
Claiming racial discrimination in
Georgia and Texas and Alabama,
Battles the insurgents lost.

After a child-filled yellow school bus
Had circled the protest encampment in Grant Park and
The children had chanted "We Want Peace"
Over and over again.

After a nervous National Guard commander
Ordered the firing of tear gas grenades, and
The gas drifted south along the lakefront
From Lincoln Park to the city's central business district, and
Delegates and demonstrators alike sought refuge
In stores and restaurants and hotel lobbies
From the fumes that assailed
Their eyes and noses and throats.

After the mayor of the Big Shoulders city
Ended the convention's second day
With an early-morning throat slash
Before the impassioned platform debate
On war and peace could begin.

After the night-time clearings of Lincoln Park
Where clubs were swung and heads were struck.

After a security man slugged a CBS reporter
On the convention floor, and an NBC correspondent
Found himself reporting from somewhere in custody.

After the convention hall had echoed
With chants of "Stop the war"
But the delegates had voted,
Sixty percent to forty percent,
To continue the war, and
A folksinger from New York,
In his delegation's isolation
At the back of the convention hall
Led hundreds in mourning
The defeat of the peace plank
With a defiant rendition of
"We Shall Overcome."

After the Mobilization,
Black and red and Viet Cong flags flying,
Set out on its funeral march
To the convention hall.

After the police, three ranks deep,
Helmeted incongruously in hardened sky-blue plastic,
Halted the marchers at the intersection of
Michigan Avenue and Balbo Drive.

After the police opened their ranks
To allow passage of the mule-drawn wagons of
The Poor People's Campaign.

After hundreds among the marchers
Hurled insults at an absent president.
"Fuck you, LBJ," they chanted.

After the thousands filling the avenue,
Eerily lit by network floodlights,
Told the police the whole world was watching.

After the police, in shirts as sky-blue as their helmets,
Galled by the insults of the marchers and
By missiles thrown from hotel windows,
Had had enough and
Charged with raised riot batons.

After the demonstrators, those who could,
Retreated before them, down side streets,
Across a bridge, into the park.

After the hard core of the demonstrators,
Ragged, scrawny, hirsute young men,

Capering, taunting dwarves,
Gesturing obscenely with arms and fingers,
Showering the police with
Accusations of incest,
Scampered away from the raised batons
In a bizarre game of tag.

After the beaten and bloody had retreated
Into the relative safety of the Hilton, and
The volunteer headquarters of the McCarthy campaign
Became of necessity a first-aid station.

After a senator from Connecticut
Dared to accuse the mayor of
Using Gestapo tactics on
The streets of the mayor's city.

After multiple Johnsonian humiliations of Hubert Humphrey
Turned the vice-president into damaged goods,
Yet culminated in his nomination for
The highest office in the gift of the American People.

II

The young woman sitting at the piano
Was slender, dark-haired, attractive,
Her arms bare in a
Sleeveless black cocktail dress,
Attired for a party
That would never be held,
The party that would have celebrated
The McCarthy nomination.

The attire gave the young woman away.
No gypsy-dressed flower-child she,
No, she worked within the system
And the system did not work,
Not for her, nor for her friends
In the McCarthy campaign.

Slowly, a key at a time,
She picked out the Dylan song,
"Come gather round people
Wherever you roam."
No need for sheet music.
She knew the song by heart,
Played it like a funeral dirge,
If not for the country itself
Then for a vision of the country
That had just died in its own small way
On Michigan Avenue,
And that was dying daily
In another, more deadly way
In rice patties and jungled hills
Half a world away.

The young woman did not know
How the changing times would end,
But she knew that history was stirring,
That the baton charges were merely
A sign of the change.

It was the end of August in 1968 and
The times, they were a-changin'.
No question there, but
For better, for worse? Who knew?
Even now, many wars later, who knows?

On Guard

Fresh out of college,
Economics major, French minor.
Decision time.
Wait for greetings from the President, or
Join the Guard.
In the end, an easy decision.
He joined the Guard.
Six months of active duty, then
Two weeks of summer camp and
A weekend a month for a term of years.
A drag, to be sure, but
Better an armory in the suburbs than
A rice paddy in the Delta,
Hunting for Victor Charlie,
Being hunted by him.

Active duty in Georgia,
At Fort McPherson, Third Army Headquarters,
The Circle A Ranch the soldiers called it,
After the shoulder patch.
George Patton long dead, but
His army still renowned,
Racing across France
In the high summer of Forty-Four,
Relieving the Screaming Eagles
At Bastogne in December.

The duty at McPherson was easy
Once his commanding officer learned that
He could shoot a basketball.

More play than work after that.
Sports a big thing in the Army.

Only one gut-tightening moment.
Detailed as prisoner-chaser,
He stood guard, shotgun in hand,
Over a dozen miscreants
Dispatched from the stockade
To pick up golf course trash.

In his mind a nagging question:
What if one of them ran?
Could he pull the trigger,
Shoot something other than a basketball?
He did not know,
Did not wish to know.

His wish became a prayer:
Please God, don't let any of them run.

God heard his prayer,
Smiled upon him, and
Was gracious to him.
No one ran.

The clean-up over,
He returned the prisoners to the stockade,
Drenched in his own perspiration,
A great weight lifting from his shoulders as
He handed over the last prisoner.

On his way back to the barracks,
He thought, strangely, of Camus,
Who also knew the absurd.

Metaphor

He stood beside the bar
With a drink in his hand
In the Kite and Key Room
Of the old Ben Franklin Hotel,
A world away from another hotel,
The Majestic, down by the river.

He spoke of the final days,
When General Giap's divisions
Approached the city.
He described the panic, the chaos,
The mobs desperate to escape,
Besieging the American Embassy.

In those final days
He carried a shaving kit everywhere, and
In the kit was a hand grenade.
If trouble erupted on
A crowded city street,
A prescribed Agency procedure:
Unzip the kit, arm the grenade,
Roll it into the crowd, and walk away.

An enduring metaphor:
America in Vietnam.

Adventuress

I

The monsoon rains came, as always at the end of April,
And they turned the trenches into canals.
The woman stood in the trench,
The water up to her hips,
The rain dripping steadily off
The brim of the coolie hat she wore over her veil,
Her flowing robes, once so pretty, so colorful,
Rose and turquoise and gold,
Soiled now, streaked with mud.
The jewelry for which her like were famous,
The bangles and baubles, the earrings and bracelets,
All had been set aside, distractions, encumbrances
In the cramped quarters of the dressing stations.

She waited to be summoned to the dugout
To attend to the wounded.
There were no wounded yet,
Not on this night,
But before long there would be.
They all knew that,
The soldiers, the doctors, and the woman alike.
The Viet gunners had the range and
Even now were shelling the camp.
And when the shelling stopped,
The Viets would rise from their own trenches
And flow forward like an army of ants
Into the fire of the French machineguns,
And though many would fall, they would keep coming,

And though they might not triumph this night,
At length they would, an army of ants, conquerors.

As the woman waited in the watery trench,
Waiting for the stretcher-bearers
To arrive with their burdens,
Waiting for the summons
To the dressing station in the dugout,
There was time to reflect
On where she was and
How she came to be there.

With the Viet shells falling around them,
With the bunkers and the trenches collapsing
Under the shellfire and the rain,
The paras and the Legionnaires
Were too busy fighting for their lives
To think it strange
That a woman from the brown Algerian hills,
From the Ouled-Nail,
Should be standing in water up to her waist
In a trench in a remote Tonkin valley.

The woman waited to be called to minister
To men who had been her customers,
Men she had pleasured.
They had been whole men
When she had pleasured them,
But now they would no longer be whole.

In the trench, as the monsoon rains fell,
And with them the shells of the Viets,
The shells that maimed and mangled and killed,
The woman thought how strange it was,

This standing in a muddy trench
As it filled with water,
This mystery in the ways of Allah,
Blessed be his name.

II

Within the tribe, the Ouled-Nail,
It was a career, an honorable career.
The girls learned to dance for men,
Learned to comfort men,
Learned to pleasure them.

And when the learning was done,
The girls were deemed to be women and
They came down from the *bled,*
Down from the brown hills,
Down to the cities,
Algiers, Oran, Constantine,
Cities where men would pay good money,
Pay for women to dance for them,
To comfort them, pleasure them.

They were frugal, these women of the Ouled-Nail,
Saving from their pay, building dowries,
And when they had built enough,
They left the cities and returned to the brown hills,
To the villages in the bled,
Women of substance now,
At least by village standards,
Able to choose among suitors,
To enter upon lives of dignity and respect,

Esteemed by most, though perhaps envied
By women who lacked their spirit of adventure.

The most adventurous of all,
The women not satisfied with life
In the brothels of the cities,
Responded to the army's call,
The invitation to dance
For paras and Legionnaires and their comrades,
To comfort them, pleasure them,
Before they set forth to risk their lives.

It was indeed a life of adventure,
In far off, exotic lands,
Wherever the army served.
Secure in its way, this life of theirs,
No want of customers,
Medical care, good pay
(From the soldiers, not the army).
A madam in charge, yes,
But better a madam
Than the pimps of the cities.

Thus they came to Tonkin,
These adventurous women of the Ouled-Nail,
To this mountainous land of little yellow people.
First to Lai-Chau in the T'ai country, and then,
When the French abandoned the post,
To the fortified camp
In the valley of the Nam Youm,
The place they called Dien Bien Phu.

The men of the garrison welcomed the girls,
Dug an underground bunker for them

Into the reverse slope of the hill
The French had named Dominique.

In those early days, the war seemed remote.
The women sunned themselves
On the banks of the Nam Youm,
Bought fruit and vegetables
In the villages of the valley.
In the evenings, when no customers appeared,
The women danced for themselves,
With arms outstretched, in flowing robes,
The tribe's music playing on a scratchy record,
The record spinning on an ancient turntable
Powered by a whirring generator next to the bunker.
The dance was mesmerizing, carrying the dancers
Away, into a world of dreams,
A world beyond the valley of the Nam Youm.

The women of the Ouled-Nail
Were not alone in their profession
In the fortified camp.
Five Vietnamese women and a Chinese madam
Came from Hanoi, guests of the Legion,
Their bunker dug into a hill called Claudine.

They served as nurses too,
These Vietnamese women, but for them,
If the camp should fall,
Likely a different fate
From that of the women of the Ouled-Nail.
The Viets were puritans as well as communists.
For them, the Arab women
Were fellow victims of imperialism.
But their own women,

Those who serviced the soldiers of the imperialists,
Were traitors as well as whores.
If the camp fell, would the twittering
Of those women ever be heard again?

In Tonkin, everyone knew of the BMCs,
The Bordels Mobiles de Campagne,
But they were not publicized beyond.
The Americans were paying for the war
(though not for the self-sufficient BMCs),
And it was not hard to imagine
A puritanical member of Congress,
As puritanical as the Viets,
Taking the floor of the House
To denounce the taxpayer funding
Of even more French decadence.

III

In the beginning it had rained men.
Paras from the colonial regiments, from the Legion,
The cream of the expeditionary force,
Their parachutes drifting lazily down
Out of the November sky.
Three months later, the rain of shells began,
Cratering the earth,
Blowing the roofs off blockhouses,
Collapsing trenches.
With that deadly rain falling,
Few ventured out of the trenches.
Of necessity the trenches became latrines.
Hygiene no longer mattered.

The men of the garrison
Had other business to attend to.

After the first cascade of falling shells,
The French spoke of flying the women of the BMCs
Out of the valley of the Nam Youm.
Imprisonment in a hellhole had not been anticipated.
But within two weeks it was too late.
The Viets had found the range of the airstrip.
A plane might run the gauntlet of Viet flak
And land without incident, but moments later
Its presence brought a barrage
And no plane could survive
The bursting shells long enough
To load a dozen wounded or
The women of the BMCs and
Lift its cargo to safety.
The Viets blocked all other exits from the valley.
The women of the BMCs were there for the duration.

But if there was no way out,
There was a way in.
Night after night, some jumping for the first time,
Volunteers parachuted into the fortified camp,
Replacing the dead and wounded of the garrison,
Knowing that death or capture was their likely fate.
Brave men, these were.
Worthy successors to the Frenchmen
Who had fought at Marengo and Austerlitz,
At Wagram and Waterloo,
At Camerone and Verdun and Bir Hakeim.
The women of the BMCs admired their courage,
These brave *gars,*
But questioned their good sense.

IV

The smells were sickening.
Above ground they came from
The hundreds of Viet bodies,
Unburied, rotting like overripe fruit,
Swarming with flies.
Underground in the dressing stations,
The smells were more complex,
But just as sickening,
Compounded of odors from unwashed bodies,
From blood and vomit,
From urine and feces.
Underground too was the kingdom of the maggots.
They swarmed as well,
Over blankets and sheets,
Bandages and plaster casts.

Le merdier, the men came to call the base,
The chamber pot, the toilet bowl, and
Ultimately, the shithole.
After the rains began in mid-April,
Replacing the drizzle the Viets called the *Crachin,*
When the full force of the monsoon struck two weeks later,
The base came to resemble a scene from an earlier war,
A blasted, devastated landscape,
Water filling the shellholes and the bomb craters,
Rising three feet and more in the communications trenches.

A thousand, even two thousand
Of the defenders quit.
Mainly Vietnamese and North African,
Perhaps they sensed that
This was not their war.

They dug themselves caves
In the banks of the river.
"The Rats of the Nam Youm,"
They were called.
They came out in the night
To scavenge for food
Among the air-dropped supply bundles.
The French let them be.
Why waste energy and ammunition on them?
The women of the BMCs scorned them
For not doing their part.

V

They had prepared for wounded,
Even hundreds of wounded.
They had brought in doctors, male nurses,
One surgical team after another,
Ready to treat, ready to operate,
But they had not prepared
For the thousands of bursting Viet shells,
And so they were not prepared
For the thousands of wounded
The shells would cause.

After a month of shelling,
Of human wave assaults,
The thousands of wounded
Had overwhelmed the medical teams.
The chief doctor needed more nurses.
Desperate, he approached the women of the BMCs.
To his relief, most volunteered
To bring comfort of a different sort

To the men of the garrison.
Business had fallen off anyway.

VI

The rain continued to fall on the woman in the trench.
She thought of her life,
Providing services to men,
Dancing and sex, for a price.
Now she would provide other services,
To men without eyes, without jaws,
Without arms, without legs,
Men with the gray ropes of their bowels
Spilling out of their stomachs,
Men whose minds the shelling had taken.
For no price at all
She would nurse these men,
Her comforting of them
No longer a matter of commerce.

Her part was acceptance.
It was what Allah had written.
She thought of the future,
If she lived to have a future.
(The shells had not discriminated.
Four of the Ouled-Nail had died under them.)
There was a man,
Algerian like herself,
A customer at first,
But there was an attraction between them,
No longer merely a matter of commerce.
He was competent, a builder of bunkers.

He could support her once this adventure ended.
She would have her dowry too, and
There could be children.
That would be good.
Life after so much death.

Someone pulled back the blanket
Covering the entrance to the dressing station.
The doctor, stripped to the waist,
His chest glistening with sweat,
Appeared in the entrance, beckoning.
"Come," he said, "you are needed now."
The woman could hear the fatigue in his voice.
Wading through the muddy, waist-high water,
She entered the arena of agony.

IV. MINDFUL

February Mist

A late winter storm
Spreads across half the nation,
Affecting tens of millions.
In the Midwest, on the Great Plains,
The storm piles the snow
In drifts six feet deep,
Stranding motorists,
Cancelling flights,
Dominating the news.

In and around the nation's capital,
The weather is grim, but less severe,
The temperature hovering near forty,
The moisture in the air more mist than rain.
Yet another chill, damp, February Saturday.

But below ground, in a suburban Metro station,
The atmosphere is festive.
The station's great, gray,
Ill-lit, vaulted cavern
Is seldom a cheerful place,
But today it is alive, loud, bustling.
With a hockey game downtown,
The station is awash in red,
Red caps, red jackets, red jerseys.
Hockey fans jam the platforms,
Crowd into the subway cars.
Optimism prevails.
Game time is still an hour away.

Downtown, a few blocks from the arena,
The atmosphere is different.

The streets are wet, slick, nearly deserted.
The rare pedestrians hobble like hunchbacks,
Crouching with faces covered
Against the skin-stinging mist.

In front of a McDonald's,
A burly man shuffles in place,
Panhandling with a paper cup.
The man talks only to himself.
He must be chilled,
This man with a paper cup.
No overhanging roof
Protects him from the mist.

The office building is closed for the weekend,
But in the alcove of the building's doorway,
A man sleeps, a big man,
Bulking large under layered blankets
Of coarse, purple-gray wool.
He is not the only man
Sheltering in a downtown doorway
Beside a mist-wet sidewalk.

Below ground, the rumbling subway trains
Deliver the hockey fans to the arena.
Soon enough, jubilation reigns
In the triple-tiered stands.
They had hoped for a hat trick
From an all-star, and they got one.

No hat tricks outside McDonald's.
None in the office building's doorway alcove.

Bargain Hunters

It is early on a Thursday morning,
And the great weekly scavenger hunt resumes.
In their battered and aged pickup trucks
Small brown hooded men
Prowl the suburban neighborhoods of
One of America's richest counties.

Their hunt must begin in darkness because
Three waves of county trucks
Will be coming soon
For the yard waste,
The fallen leaves and broken branches,
For the recycling,
The paper and plastic and glass and tin,
And finally for the trash itself.

They have come from the south,
These small brown men,
From Mexico and Salvador and Guatemala,
And they have learned that the streets
Are not paved with gold, but
They have also learned that
Small windfalls can appear at lawn edges,
The no longer wanted,
Perhaps never needed
Stuff of the American middle class.

Tables and chairs and three-wheeled bikes,
Clock radios and television sets,
Toasters and microwaves,

Even the insulated copper wires that
Tied the electronic devices to power.

For the hunters who deal
In scrap metal, there is
The occasional jackpot,
A big gas grill that has
Outlived its usefulness.

To wrestle a big gas grill
Into the bed of a pickup truck
At six o'clock on a Thursday morning,
That is the making of
A very good day.

Responding

Friday morning, the sun bright overhead
In a cerulean sky, in sharp contrast
To the overcast Monday before,
When lights-blazing cruisers and ambulances
Raced to the Navy Yard.

The newly-purchased pansies,
All purple and yellow and blue,
Stand in their plastic pots,
Awaiting their replanting in the boxes
On the wall of the porch.

The woman mounts the ancient, foldable,
Two-step ladder, trowel in hand, begins to dig.
Three boxes, twenty minutes a box.
In an hour, the replanting is done.
Now for the water.
The transplanted earth must be saturated
Or the pansies will not grow.

The woman mounts the stepladder again,
Hose nozzle in hand.
The water flows, and a gentle spray
Descends upon the flowers.

But then the stepladder collapses and
The woman falls, backwards,
Onto the stone floor of the porch.
Her tailbone is the first to hit,
But it does not keep her head

From cracking against the stone.
Blood begins to flow.

Inside the house, in the kitchen,
A clumsy effort at first aid.
Water-soaked paper towels,
Gauze pads, a makeshift icebag.
The blood is bright red, streaming.
Cadmium red, an artist would call it.
The color leaps off the wet towels, the gauze pads
When they are lifted from the head-gash.
The woman's hair is gray, silvery even,
But the drying blood has darkened it
To the artist's alizarin crimson.

What did they see, those Monday first-responders,
When they entered Building 197 and
Came upon the carnage scene?
They saw blood too, so much of it,
From twelve gunshot-violated bodies.
Was it is still bright red, or was it darkening?
No matter. Too late for gauze pads or wetted towels.

Mindful

It is early afternoon, and
The traffic lanes on the boulevard,
The two not taken up by parked cars,
Are flowing smoothly.
One of the motorists is bound for a bookstore,
Hoping to find on its shelves
A widely-praised guide to
The practice of mindfulness.

Ahead, on the right,
A man emerges from the space
Between two parked cars.
He is in the middle of the block.
No pedestrian crosswalk there, but no matter.
He gazes calmly at the two lanes of traffic
Bearing down on him, but
The oncoming cars seem not to register with him.

Undaunted, uncomprehending,
He begins to cross the street.
Four cars back, the book-hunting driver
Can scarcely believe his eyes.

The man on foot is fortunate,
For no car strikes him.
Instead, he strikes a car,
Striding squarely into its side as it passes.
He reels backwards, away from his collision
With the car's indifferent and unyielding metal.
He crumples to the ground
As cars come to screeching halts around him.

A young woman darts out from the sidewalk,
Crouches near him, retrieves the shopping bag
He dropped as he fell.

The bookstore-bound motorist pulls off the road
Beyond the man on the ground,
Turns on his flashers,
Walks back to where
The fallen man struggles to his feet,
Accepts the bag the young woman offers and
Begins to walk unsteadily away.

The motorist overtakes him,
Asks if he is all right.
"I think so," the man says, and
Continues across the street,
Through the jumble of hastily-halted cars.
For him, the conversation is over.

With nothing to be done,
The motorist returns perplexed to his car,
Sure now that he is not the only one in need of
A book on mindfulness.

Saturday Night at California Tortilla

It is Saturday night at California Tortilla,
A thin stream of customers trickling in.
Outside it is cold and damp,
Mist hanging in the air,
The streets wet from an earlier rain.

Inside, the store is new,
Moved from across the street, roomier, airier,
With a new color scheme,
More guacamole than red bean,
A new menu to match,
Though the tacos and burritos are unchanged.

An old woman enters,
Thick of body, full of face.
Her hair is long and gray,
Roughly combed if combed at all.
Her coat, long and black and soiled and coarse,
Might have been a horse blanket.

She supports herself with a walker,
A fancy walker, with thin rubber tires
And handbrakes on the handles,
Like a better brand of bicycle.

She steers the walker to a counter
Where bored young men
In T-shirts and baseball caps
The color of guacamole
Wait behind cash registers.

She places her order with one bored young man,
Who passes it on to the Latinas
Who work assembly-line style
Behind a glass-fronted counter,
Scooping rice and beans and chicken and
Beef and pork and salsa and queso and lettuce
Onto platters and tacos and burritos.

As her order moves down the line,
The woman takes her empty drink cup and
Steers the walker to the drinks machine,
The latest generation thereof,
A stand-alone soda fountain,
With buttons for more than a dozen options,
Colas diet and regular,
Lemonade and orangeade,
Root beer and cream soda,
Even mysterious imports from health food stores.

The woman hesitates, bewildered,
The sheer variety of options too much for her.
Behind her, teenagers fidget,
Willing the woman to make a choice, move on.

At last the choice is made,
A button pushed, the drink drawn.
On the other side of the store,
The woman's order number is called.
The steering of the walker resumes.

A moment of confusion.
There has been a mistake.
Her order sits on a tray, ready to be eaten,
But she ordered carry-out.

The Latinas swiftly adjust, the tray is unloaded,
The food transferred to a plastic bag,
The woman's drink cup inserted,
The bag handles tied together for ease of handling.

The woman accepts the bag and
Turns the walker towards the nearest door.

One hand awkwardly clutches the ties on the bag and
Tries to help with the walker's steering.
It is not much help.
The walker lurches across the floor.

The woman reaches the door, alone.
No one is near to hold the door for her.
She begins to push through it, but
The walker snags on the doorframe.

The woman wedges her broad, thick body
Between the door and the walker.
She wrestles the walker through the doorway
Onto the sidewalk beyond.

The mist still hangs in the air.
The woman turns the fancy walker once again,
Sets off up the rain-wet street.
A continuing struggle, a small victory.

Saturday night at California Tortilla.

Island Men

They stand on traffic islands at major intersections,
Next to the left-turn lane,
The better to approach motorists
Stopped and waiting for the green arrow.
They are older men, forty and beyond,
Black and white, unshaven, likely unwashed,
Shabby clothing soiled and sweat-stained.

They hold crude, creased cardboard signs,
Hand-lettered, clumsily, with Magic Markers,
The messages sounding variations on familiar themes:
"Disabled," "Homeless," "Jobless," "Hungry,"
"Vietnam veteran," "Please help."
In this pleasant, leafy suburb,
Neighbor to the capital of the free world,
Not all have prospered.

No independent contractors, these island men.
No, they are organized.
Witnesses have seen the van.
It pulls up in the morning,
Drops them off, one to an island,
With backpack and water bottle,
Ready for a long day's soliciting.
In the afternoon, the van returns,
Picks them up and drives off,
The day's proceeds to be divided later.

What is it like, inside their heads,
These island men? Inside their souls?

A lifetime of dreams, of hopes,
Of ambitions, experiences,
Shrunken in middle age
To this solitary daily vigil
On a suburban traffic island,
Dependent, like Blanche Dubois,
On the kindness of strangers.

Weeping

Sunday morning at the parish church,
The eight-thirty Mass over,
The congregation dismissed,
The final hymn ended,
The worshippers drift
Towards the vestibule
Where the ushers wait
To distribute the parish bulletin,
And beyond them the priest-celebrant
Is poised to greet his flock.

Three-quarters of the way down the center aisle,
Ten pews from the back of the church,
A thirtyish woman remains in her pew
In the familiar Catholic crouch,
Half-sitting, half-kneeling,
Her head inclined forward, her arms
Extended over the back of the pew in front.
She is weeping, silently, copiously,
The tears raining down from her angled face,
Onto the bench in front of her,
Puddling, there are so many.

Perhaps they are tears of joy,
But no, there is no joy in her face.
Tears of sorrow or grief then,
Surely one of these,
A surge of sorrow or grief so intense
That she does not care
Who sees her or what they think,

Her fellow worshippers,
These middle-class suburbanites,
Wending their way home
To substantial breakfasts and the Sunday papers.

Why does this woman weep,
This woman alone in her world of pain:
Loss of a loved one, a child perhaps,
Loss of innocence, of happiness,
Of the self that once was hers,
The person she once was,
A person she can never recover?
Her tears a sign that beyond the Mass,
Beneath its rituals, its routines,
There lurks the serious business of life,
Even the serious business of death.

Why does this woman weep?
The answer to the question
Is known only to her as she crouches alone
In this slowly emptying church,
Surrounded by strangers.

Charade

A vacation for the extended family,
A lakeside rental in Vermont,
A broad back lawn
Sloping gently down to the water
Where the kayaks bob rhythmically
On the wavelets.

The woman stands alone, smoking,
On the deck above the lawn,
Looking out over the rippled gray-green lake
Where the Sea-Doos and the Jet Skis buzz
Like angry hornets and
Cut great curving wakes through the water.

Below the woman, on the lawn,
Her brother, her husband, her two sons,
Toss beanbags at a hole in a tilted plank.
There is much commotion,
Shouting and laughter,
Cheering and applause.

The woman, standing alone, smoking,
Knows it for a charade.
Her husband, the father of her sons,
Has another woman
Back at their home, in New Hampshire.
She knows that, but he
Does not know that she knows,
And so the charade continues.

The woman thinks back to her wedding,
Ten years in the past,
A bright October Saturday on the Maine coast,
The big tent on the hotel lawn,
The parquet dance floor atop the grass,

The bar open and busy,
The ocean a hundred yards away,
The sea breeze, tangy with the smell of the Atlantic,
Coming off the water,
Family and friends stomping to the DJ's music.
Congratulations, hugs,
Kisses, all around.
So much promise.

She stands alone on the deck, smoking.
The smoking is not good for her,
She knows that,
But it calms her, and
So she continues to smoke.

She turns her gaze
From the watercraft out on the lake
To the lawn below her,
To the latest act in the charade
As it plays out.
So much promise.

Euphoria fades, day by day.
Years pass, and then
It is gone for good.

V. PILGRIMAGE

Into the Pyrenees

A venture into the unknown,
The Basque countryside and
The low peaks of the western Pyrenees,
The familiar scenes of the City of Light,
Eiffel's tower, a triumphal arch, Notre Dame,
Hundreds of kilometers behind.

The car is an Opel Corsa,
A fine little vehicle once you learn
To squeeze the button on the stick
To put the car in reverse.

The road winds south,
Out of the village,
La Bastide Clairence,
"One of the most beautiful in France,"
The tourist maps say,
Past the gift shops,
The awning-shaded bistros,
The ancient parish church
With its grim, gray stone panel
Bearing the names of the parish's dead
In the Great War.

The road leads narrowly past small farms
With weathered cottages,
Sagging barns, hedge-rowed fields,
Roughly fenced and stubbled pastures,
On through other Basque villages

Less picturesque than La Bastide –
Hasparren, Bonloc, Helette, Irissarry.

Gradually the road rises
Into the foothills of the Pyrenees,
No farms here, all rock-strewn pasture now,
A few scattered, stunted trees,
And in the pastures, the belled, pale-hided beef cattle,
The Blondes d'Aquitaine,
That roam grazing across them,
The tinkling of their bells inaudible
So long as the Corsa is in motion.

The road curls higher and higher,
Along the shoulders of the hills,
Still paved, but less wide,
Room for only a single car.

Off to the right, higher on the hillside,
A solitary boulder-perched birder
Armed with binoculars and camera
Watches a single buzzard
Drift lazily across the sky.

The driver slows the Corsa,
Pulls off to the side of the road,
Turns off the engine.
He and his passenger leave the car,
Walk to the downhill edge of the road
Where the land drops steeply away,
Affords a distant view
Of the winding valleys
Hundreds of meters below,

Their toy villages and farms,
The red-roofed, white-walled cottages,
Linked by slender gray ribbons of road,
The roads flanked by muted
Green and brown patches of landscape,
Narrow green fingers of forest
Reaching down the hillsides from the heights above.

In the distance the hills are purple and blue,
A creamy haze washing over them,
While above, thin pale gray clouds
Race across the sky.

The heights are strangely warm in early September,
Immensely quiet too, the only sound
The faint, distant tinkling of cowbells, now audible
As their bearers high-step across the grassy hillsides
Like parading show horses.

At length, the scene observed, the photos taken,
The driver and the passenger regain the Corsa,
Begin their descent,
The car following the curving road
Down the hill's now sloping shoulder
To the flatlands below,
The River Nive and Saint-Jean-Pied-de-Port,
Last stop in France
For pilgrims on the Way of Saint James,
Their goal the great shrine of the Apostle
At Compostela, in far northwest Spain.

The pilgrims who come here will use
Pied-de-Port, The Foot of the Pass,

And a famous pass it is –
Roncevaux, the French call it.
Charlemagne, Roland, Oliver,
The evil Ganelon, thousands of Saracen warriors,
All of them passed this way,
More than a millennium ago,
Or so Roland's own Song has it.

In the town, on the winding, cobble-stoned streets,
Rising and falling with the shape of the land,
The pilgrims, hunchbacked and more
Beneath their mammoth rucksacks,
Pose smiling for camera-wielding tourists.

The return across the lowlands to La Bastide
is uneventful, but etched in memory
The breath-catching view
Across the valleys
To the haze-shrouded hills.
Alive in memory too
The delicate tinkling of the bells
Worn by the Blondes d'Aquitaine
As the cream-skinned cattle pranced across
The hillside pastures of the Pays Basque.

Visiting Saint-Sulpice

At Saint-Sulpice,
Church of mismatched towers,
A memorial Mass has just ended,
The mourners clustered in small groups
On the broad, sunlit plaza
In front of the church
Near the monumental Fountain of the Four Bishops,
The plaza bordered by tree-lined sidewalks,
Elegant shops, crowded cafes.

To enter the church is to move
From daylight to semi-darkness,
Where the air is alive with organ music.
No matter that the Mass is over,
The organist continues to play,
His mammoth instrument,
With its five keyboards,
The grandest in Europe.

Beyond the entrance,
Flanking the center aisle,
Two enormous half-clamshells:
Outsized gifts from a fabled city on the Adriatic,
Serving now as fonts for holy water.

Off to the right,
The Chapel of the Holy Angels.
Delacroix worked here,
Painting two giant murals,
Scenes from Genesis and Second Maccabees,

Jacob grappling with one angel,
Two others driving Heliodorus from Jerusalem's Temple.

On the floor of the nave, the famous gnomon,
The one that tourists, readers of a famous novel,
Come to see, but the brass strip leading to the obelisk,
Catching rays of sunlight,
Tells only of solstices and equinoxes,
Not Priories of Sion.

On either side of the nave,
Beneath the soaring, many-vaulted ceiling,
A museum's worth of statuary
In front of the supporting columns.

Behind the main altar,
The Lady Chapel,
The floodlit statue of Madonna and Child
Aglow in pink marble.

Beyond the columns on both sides,
Broad aisles lead past side chapels,
A dozen or more,
Named after long-dead saints,
Some fronted by banks of flickering candles,
Evidence of lingering devotion
In the Church's eldest daughter,
Even as the tide of secularism
Continues its inexorable advance.

At length a side chapel
So dimly-lit it is easily overlooked.
Mort pour la France,

The inscription on a wall says,
And on gray stone panel
After gray stone panel,
Beneath and beside it
As the chapel's other walls
Wrap around the altar,
Columns of names descend,
Men of the parish, hundreds of them,
Who died for France in the War
To End All Wars.

Behind the names, of necessity
Hundreds of families,
Spouses, children, parents,
Left in desolation
As industrial-scale warfare
On the Marne, the Meuse, the Somme,
In the Artois and at Verdun,
On the Chemin des Dames,
Turned the Luxembourg Quarter
Into a vast plain of mourning.

The panels echo other names,
Those inscribed on the mass graves
That lie to the east,
Dotting the French and Belgian countrysides
From the North Sea to Switzerland,
The Western Front,
Where the butchery took place.

The panels serve too as
Mute witness to the exhaustion
That left the nation too war-weary to resist
When the Germans marched again.

Visitors depart, and the murals and clamshells,
The statuary and the gnomon,
They fade from memory,
But the panels, the long columns of names remain,
A somber reminder that
There is more to this church and its history,
More to France and its history,
More to life itself
Than Fodor's tells the tourist.

VI. SADDEST WORDS

Billowing Overcoats

Prayers have been read,
Oaths taken,
Speeches given,
Anthems sung,
Lunch eaten,
Ceremonial gifts offered.
The parade, already late, may begin.

A color guard, a military band,
A series of flying wedges,
Police motorcycles first,
Emergency vehicles, hazard lights ablaze, last,
The limousines sandwiched between.
Down America's Main Street they come.

The January day is cold,
Not Arctic cold, but cold enough.
On sidewalks and grandstands,
The spectators are bundled up –
Hats and gloves, parkas and scarves.

Some present are not bundled up.
A dozen, two dozen,
Hatless, scarfless, gloveless,
They walk in loose perimeters
That encircle two of the limousines.
Men and women in dark suits and overcoats,
Multi-racial, multi-ethnic,
Men in white shirts and dark ties,
Women – fewer of them – tieless.

Their overcoats, Burberry, London Fog,
Billow unbuttoned, sail-like,
In the chill January wind.
Are the wearers not cold?
Among them there is no lightness of heart.
Grim of face, they do not cease
Their crowd-scanning.

They do not mind the wind whipping at their coats –
They need instant access
To the weapons they carry under those coats,
The Sig Sauer P-Two-Twenty-Nines
Holstered on hips and under shoulders,
Rich in stopping power.
A buttoned overcoat might mean fatal delay.

At last it comes, ten blocks into the parade,
The moment of supreme anxiety
For the men and women in the billowing overcoats.

The most massive of the limousines brakes to a stop.
A man in an unbuttoned overcoat emerges, looks around.
They are always looking around,
this man and his colleagues.
He opens the back passenger-side door.
Another opens the back door on the other side.
The doors are thick, maybe the thickest ever.
The First Couple steps out.
They begin to walk, begin to wave.
The crowd is cheering now,
Women and girls screaming.
The men and women in the billowing overcoats
Walk in their own zone of stress,

Alert for an assassin
Driven by politics or madness –
Are they not related? –
Dashing out from the crowd.

Once the First Couple passes the White House,
Their winter stroll is over.
They reenter their limousine,
Disappear into the mansion grounds.
A few moments later, they emerge,
Walk down a planked gangway
To the reviewing stand.
Military units, high school bands,
Native American dancers, Canine Companions,
They all march past, and
The couple stands to applaud.

The men and women in the billowing overcoats,
Just a handful now,
Slip into second-row seats,
Behind the First and Second Couples,
In the midst of presidential family and friends.
Deep breaths taken, thin smiles on faces,
A few moments of calm
For men and women in
Unbuttoned and billowing overcoats.

Backups

The oppression and the dispossession continue.
In Israel proper, invidious discrimination.
In East Jerusalem, ethnic cleansing.
On the West Bank, apartheid.
In Gaza, an open-air concentration camp.
The United States responds forcefully.
"We have Israel's back," the President says.
The Secretary of State provides an echo.

A different time, a different place.
The mid-seventies, a federal courtroom.
The police and the FBI have caught up with them,
This amateurish crew of North Philadelphia robbers.
An alert teller pushing an unseen button,
A dye-pack bursting in a bag of bills –
Whatever the means, they are well and truly caught.
Some look for leniency, agree to plead guilty,
Cooperate with the government,
Testify against their confederates.
Others, the fools, take their chance with a jury.

He is a small man, dapper in a light gray three-piece suit,
Pleased to be the center of attention.
He is a witness for the United States, and
He is eager to testify.
Years in federal prison hang in the balance.
The prosecutor asks:
"What part did you play in the robberies?"
"I waited in the getaway car.
I had the shotgun. In case of trouble."

(On the witness stand, a Philadelphia detective
Had racked the shotgun, startling a drowsy courtroom.)
"Your relationship to the gang's leader,
How would you describe it?"
He straightens in his chair, takes a deep breath.
"I was his backup man," he says proudly.
"With the shotgun."

Decades later, different crimes.
Another backup man, a backup woman too.

Tribute

A Monday night in February,
The Verizon Center three-quarters full.
Notre Dame is in town,
But the Fighting Irish have left their game
Back in northern Indiana.
Georgetown's Hoyas, long, lean, limber,
Take them to school.

Midway through the second half,
The margin reaches twenty.
Hundreds begin the trek upwards,
From their seats to the exit portals.

A pass sails out of bounds, and a whistle blows.
From the scorer's table, a signal to the referees.
A commercial imperative, a television timeout.

As the teams withdraw to their benches,
A line of people emerges from an aisle
Near the Georgetown student section,
Files onto the court,
Mostly young men, a few young women.

The men, it turns out, are wounded veterans
From America's Twenty First Century wars;
The women escort the more grievously hurt.
No athletes there, so many of them maimed,
Missing an arm, a leg, even both legs.
They hobble on crutches, propel wheelchairs.
Their artificial limbs, silvery tubes

Suitable for Star Wars robots,
Gleam in the bright arena lights.

Some of the men are unmaimed,
But their frozen faces suggest deep injuries within,
To the brain, to the soul, hidden wounds that lead to
Depression and addiction and suicide.

The public address announcer directs the crowd's attention
To the file of veterans and their escorts,
Now arranged in a ragged line at mid-court.
He identifies the veterans, names the conflicts
In which they received their wounds.
Noble abstractions, those names, floating in the ether
Above the sand and the heat and the makeshift bombs.
They are honored guests of Georgetown, the announcer says.
He requests a round of applause,
In recognition of their service, their sacrifice.

He makes no reference to the armchair Napoleons,
The think-tank field marshals
Who sent the young men on the court
To places they would call the Sandbox and the Stan,
Where the earth erupted beneath them
In truly great balls of fire and pillars of oily smoke,
Splintering bone, shredding flesh.

The dwindling crowd rises dutifully to its feet,
begins to applaud.
The veterans and escorts, curiously vulnerable,
Stand at mid-court as the applause washes over them.

After ten seconds or so, the applause begins to fade,
Dies out. It has been polite, not too long, not too loud.
Roars following pretty Georgetown baskets have been louder.

For a while, the veterans and escorts linger at mid-court,
As if waiting for something else, but there is nothing else.
At length they realize: the tribute is over.
They turn and straggle off the court,
Retracing the route they took when entering,
Enveloped by anti-climax.

As the last of the file clears the court, a horn sounds.
The players leave their sideline huddles.
The Georgetown cheerleaders begin a new set of acrobatics.
Georgetown's bulldog mascot mangles a shoebox
Labeled "Notre Dame."
Another signal from the scorer's table.
The commercials have ended, for a while at least.
The referees blow their whistles.
Play may now resume.

Gun Return

My father found his when his father died.
My brother his when his father-in-law died.

You are clearing out the dead person's home and
There it is, wrapped in a towel,
Under a stack of shirts in a drawer or
Tucked away on a shelf in a closet,
A handgun you never knew existed.
You would rather not know why it was there, but
You accept its presence, and you move on.
You cannot leave it where you found it, so
You bring it home, wrap it in another towel,
Tuck it away in another drawer or another closet,
Largely forget about it
Until something causes you to remember.

Sirhan Sirhan guns down Bobby Kennedy
In a kitchen passage at a Los Angeles hotel.
You remember the gun and
You decide you don't want it around.
You take one of your sons and
The towel-wrapped gun to the local precinct,
Where the desk sergeant is pleased to receive it,
No questions asked, and you in turn are well pleased
To walk home without it.

You and your wife decide to downsize,
Move away from your home of thirty-eight years.
As you pack for the move,
You come across the gun,

Untouched since your father-in-law's death.
It occurs to you that
It need not come with you.

And so you and your wife take the gun,
As your father has taken a gun before you,
To your local police station.
The desk sergeant is more curious,
Wanting to know your father-in-law's name,
Why he had the gun.
You really do not need
This small-time inquisition.
You just want to be rid of the goddamned thing,
But your wife is patient and explains anyway:
Her father tended bar part-time
In a tough neighborhood in South Philly.
It is enough for the sergeant.
He accepts the gun, writes out a receipt.
You leave the station house
Like others who turn in family firearms,
Relieved of a burden
You were not fully aware that you carried.

Saddest Words

I

It is the newest section,
This Section 60.

Not all the graves have headstones yet,
But they will. It is a matter of time.

On some graves, the burnt-orange earth is freshly turned.
On others, scatters of pale green grass have just begun to grow.
At the heads of some,
Flowers, in bouquets and wreaths and vases,
Flowers, arranged in red and white and blue,
Flowers, some fresh, some dying.

Small flags flutter, bend in breezes.
They too are red and white and blue.

Home from the Sandbox, home from the Stan,
The soldiers and marines are now at rest.

II

Earlier, yet another spate of childish political spite.
The government is shut down.
Protocols governing White House behavior
Are suspended, and informality prevails.
The President sits down to pizza
With junior staff members.

In a private moment,
The President and a young woman are alone.
A sexual favor is arranged and conferred.

What was he thinking?
What was he thinking with?
Was he thinking at all?

In a few days the government reopens,
Distance is reestablished,
But not between the President and the intern.

The initial encounter is repeated,
Several times.
A romance? An affair?
It does not matter.
As the oracles say,
What goes around comes around.
No one yet knows it,
But the political time bomb
Has begun its ticking.

There is a lawsuit, and
At its center, an allegation of
Another, earlier sexual encounter.
In the lawsuit, a discovery process, and
In that process, a deposition, and
In the deposition, the President is questioned
About the young woman.
Under oath, he lies.
The political explosion now only
A matter of time.

III

But imagine that on the night of the pizza,
The President declines the offered favor,
Settles instead for a pizza slice,
Pepperoni-topped, and no affair begins.

Thus there is no occasion for
The young woman to confide in a co-worker
About the affair's progress (or lack thereof),
No occasion for this co-worker
To pass this information along
To the President's political enemies.
No occasion for those enemies
To question the President
About an affair that never began.
No occasion for the President
To lie under oath.
No occasion for an independent counsel
To find grounds for impeachment.
No occasion for the House of Representatives
To return articles of impeachment.
No occasion for the Senate
To try the President
For high crimes and misdemeanors.
No occasion in the next presidential campaign
For the candidate of the opposing party –
A man who has skated though life
On the grease of family connections,
A man born on third base who believes
(Against all evidence)
That he has gotten there on his own –
To travel the country pledging to restore
Dignity and honor to the Oval Office.

No occasion for thousands of Floridians
To be so offended by presidential tawdriness
That they vote for the man born on third base.

IV

Imagine further that with a different election outcome,
The new President –
a man not without family connections of his own,
But more mature, more responsible,
Less reckless, less deluded about his own abilities –
Takes seriously the warnings of his intelligence agencies
About a Saudi Arabian fanatic and
His declaration of war.
The President puts those agencies on alert,
Orders the sharing of intelligence.
Those agencies concentrate on a man
In custody in Minnesota for immigration violations,
A flight school student who wants to learn
How to fly large jetliners, but not how to land them.
That concentration foils the greatest jihadist plot of all,
Keeps the hijackers from even boarding the planes,
And thus saves three thousand lives,
Removes any reason for
The invasion of Afghanistan,
With its attendant thousands of casualties,
American and Afghan,
Removes any reason for
The invasion of Iraq,
With its attendant thousands of casualties,
American and Iraqi, and
Removes any reason for
Cemetery officials to open Section 60.

V

In Section 60, the burial stream has slowed,
A trickle now, but still flowing,
One or two a week.

The color guard,
A platoon of marching soldiers,
A dirge-playing military band,
The flag-draped coffin on the caisson,
Drawn by six black horses, matched, prancing,
The mourners trailing behind.

At the gravesite, the mounded earth lies
Beside the opened ground.
A chaplain prays,
Soldiers fire volleys,
A bugler plays taps.

The pallbearers lift the flag from the coffin,
Stretch it taut, fold it into
A compact cloth triangle.
A general presents the flag
With too-practiced words of comfort
To the grieving spouse or the grieving parents.
And then it is over.

The mourners disperse,
The soldiers march back to their barracks,
The horses are led to their stables,
There to await the next summons to the cemetery.

In the air behind them, behind
The departing mourners and soldiers,

A feeling lingers, unvoiced,
So painful a feeling that
No one dares voice it.
It has been growing
For a decade, this feeling.
The solemn scene, the solemn ceremony,
They have revived it,
The feeling that
These burials did not have to be.

ABOUT THE AUTHOR

B orn in 1938, Tom grew up in South Philadelphia. He attend-
ed St. Joseph's Prep, Philadelphia's Jesuit high school, and the
University of Notre Dame, both on academic scholarships. Af-
ter graduating magna cum laude from Notre Dame in 1960, Tom
joined the Jesuits, where he spent most of the next eighteen years.
Along the way he was ordained a priest in 1970; acquired graduate
degrees in philosophy, English, theology and law; taught in high
school, college, and law school; helped to edit the Jesuit magazine
America; clerked for a federal judge; and served as staff counsel for
a congressional committee investigating the assassination of Dr.
Martin Luther King, Jr.

Tom left the Jesuits and the priesthood on good terms in 1978.
Shortly thereafter he married Ann Dunleavy, having first met her
on a blind date when they were college freshmen in 1956. Tom
then worked as an attorney in private practice, served as general
counsel to a government relations firm, and eventually entered
upon a seventeen-year career as an appellate attorney in the Crimi-
nal Division of the Department of Justice, during which time he
argued approximately sixty-five cases before federal circuit courts
of appeals.

Following his retirement from the Department of Justice in 2007,
he took a long-delayed plunge into the fine arts, which culminat-
ed in a solo 2012 show of fifty-four paintings and drawings at the
Yellow Barn Studio and Gallery in Glen Echo, Maryland. Finally,
after writing millions of words of dubious aesthetic value as a jour-
nalist and attorney, he began to write poetry seriously in 2013.
This volume is the result. Tom hopes there will be more to come.

Tom and Ann live in Bethesda, Maryland. Their two grown chil-
dren, Mark and Kate, live in Washington, D.C., where both are
attorneys.

This book is set in Garamond Premier Pro, which had its genesis in 1988 when type-designer Robert Slimbach visited the Plantin-Moretus Museum in Antwerp, Belgium, to study its collection of Claude Garamond's metal punches and typefaces. During the mid-fifteen hundreds, Garamond—a Parisian punch-cutter—produced a refined array of book types that combined an unprecedented degree of balance and elegance, for centuries standing as the pinnacle of beauty and practicality in type-founding. Slimbach has created an entirely new interpretation based on Garamond's designs and on compatible italics cut by Robert Granjon, Garamond's contemporary.

To order additional copies of this book
or other Antrim House titles, contact the publisher at

Antrim House
21 Goodrich Rd., Simsbury, CT 06070
860.217.0023, AntrimHouse@comcast.net
or the house website (www.AntrimHouseBooks.com).

•

On the house website
in addition to information on books
you will find sample poems, upcoming events,
and a "seminar room" featuring supplemental biography,
notes, images, poems, reviews, and
writing suggestions.